W9-BPR-168

AMAZING SHARKS!

WRITTEN BY
Sarah L. Thomson

PHOTOGRAPHS PROVIDED BY THE
Wildlife Conservation Society

WILDLIFE
CONSERVATION
SOCIETY

SCHOLASTIC INC.
New York Toronto London Auckland Sydney
Mexico City New Delhi Hong Kong Buenos Aires

There are more than 350

different kinds of sharks.

Some are as long as a fire truck.

Some are so small

you could hold one in your hand.

Some sharks have dull teeth.

Others have teeth so sharp

they can take a bite

out of a turtle's shell.

Some sharks live in rivers.

Others hide on the ocean bottom

or swim in deep water.

Some sharks even glow in the dark.

Almost all sharks are hunters.

Animals that hunt

are called predators.

(Say it like this: PRED-uh-tors.)

The white shark is a predator.

It attacks from below

to kill its favorite food—

seals or sea lions.

These animals are called its prey.

(It sounds the same as PRAY.)

A white shark can grow
as long as a pickup truck.
A whale shark can be as
long as two white sharks!
Its mouth can be wider
than your front door.

It is the biggest fish in the world.

But it eats mostly tiny animals

smaller than your fingernail.

The angel shark

hides under the sand

and waits for a fish to swim by.

Then the shark rushes out to eat it.

The cookie-cutter shark

takes just one bite out of a fish,

a whale, or a seal.

The bite is round, like a cookie.

Then the shark swims away.

angel shark

Sharks are fish,
but they are different
from other fish.
Other fish have bones.

A shark's skeleton is cartilage.

(Say it like this: CAR-til-idj.)

Your ears and nose

are made of cartilage.

It bends more easily than bone.

A shark can bend and twist

to turn quickly when it is swimming.

Most fish lay eggs in the water.

Some sharks lay eggs too.

But most sharks give birth

to their babies.

Shark babies are called pups.

14

The pups live on their own.

They do not need their parents.

They stay away from older sharks.

Some older sharks will eat pups

if they get the chance.

15

Some sharks eat stingrays

or spiny sea urchins.

Many eat other sharks.

Tiger sharks have eaten tin cans

and metal wire!

Sharks have rows

and rows of teeth.

If one tooth falls out,

a bigger one moves up

to fill in the hole.

Some sharks lose thousands of teeth

during their lives.

Sharks have many senses
to help them find food.
A shark can hear a fish in the water
from more than a mile away.

It can smell one drop of blood
in a million drops of water.

A shark can see well underwater.
A hammerhead shark has one eye
on each end of its long head.
No one is sure why.

19

If a fish is swimming or splashing,
a shark can feel the water moving.
Sharks can also feel electricity.

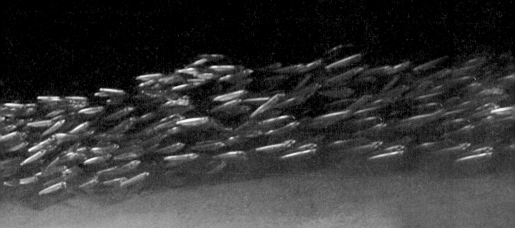

(Say it: EE-leck-TRIH-cih-tee.)

Every living thing gives off

a little bit of electricity.

People cannot feel it.

But sharks can.

Even if prey is hiding,

a shark can still find it

by feeling electricity in the water.

Many people are afraid of sharks.

But most sharks leave people alone.

You are more likely

to be hit by lightning

than to be killed by a shark.

People kill sharks every day.

They eat shark meat

or make their fins into soup.

They catch fish in huge nets.

Many sharks are killed by mistake

in these nets.

People have killed

more than half of all the sharks

in the world.

People dump trash or oil

into the ocean.

They put up buildings

near the shallow waters

where shark pups live and grow.

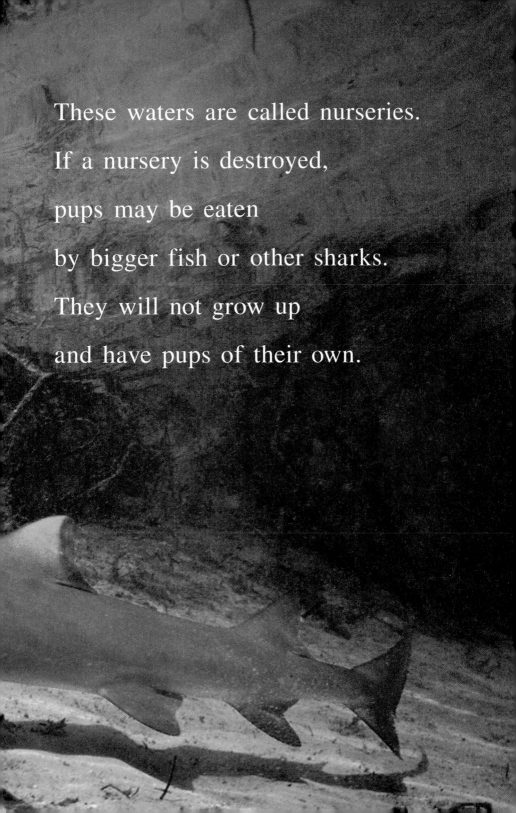

These waters are called nurseries.

If a nursery is destroyed,

pups may be eaten

by bigger fish or other sharks.

They will not grow up

and have pups of their own.

Scientists study sharks

to find out what they eat,

how far they swim,

how deep they dive,

and how many are still alive.

Sometimes they go into cages

under the water

so they can see sharks up close.

They learn how sharks live

and what they need to survive.

The ocean needs

predators like sharks.

Sharks hunt fish and other animals.

It is easiest for a shark

to catch a fish

that is weak or sick.

But strong and healthy

fish escape.

The fish lay eggs and have babies.

Their babies grow up

to be strong and healthy too.

Sharks are important
to life in the ocean.
People must find a way

to help sharks survive.

We can stop hunting sharks.

We can protect their nurseries.

AMAZING DOLPHINS!

The Wildlife Conservation Society and Dolphins

Diana Reiss, who works for the Wildlife Conservation Society (WCS), studies dolphin behavior and was one of the first scientists to tell people that dolphins were being killed in fishing nets. Brian Smith, another WCS scientist, studies river and coastal dolphins in countries such as Thailand, Bangladesh, and India. These kinds of dolphins that live closest to humans are at the greatest risk. Howard Rosenbaum's Cetacean Conservation and Research Program (CCRP) studies species like the Indo-Pacific humpback dolphin and Atlantic humpback dolphin and works with the governments of Madagascar and Gabon to ensure maximum protection for these species. WCS and other organizations are trying to keep dolphins from being killed in fishing nets, improve dolphin habitats, and change rules that make it legal to hunt dolphins.

WCS has managed the New York Aquarium for one hundred years. More than 700,000 people a year visit the aquarium to learn about marine animals such as seals, sea lions, walruses, and dolphins. To find out more about WCS and how you can help dolphins and other endangered animals, visit www.wcs.org.

With gratitude to Peter Hamilton. Special thanks to Dr. Diana Reiss, WCS scientist, dolphin expert, and consultant.
Thanks for photographs to Wildlife Conservation Society (cover, title page, 10-11, 14-15),
Marty Snyderman (4-5, 6-7, 9, 12-13, 18, 20-21, 22-23, 27, 28-29, 30-31), as well as Samuel Hung/HKDCS (17),
D. Pearlman (24-25), Diane Shapiro (32), and Brandon D. Cole.

I Can Read!

READING **2** WITH HELP

AMAZING DOLPHINS!

Written by
Sarah L. Thomson

Photographs provided by the
Wildlife Conservation Society

WILDLIFE
CONSERVATION
SOCIETY

SCHOLASTIC INC.
New York   Toronto   London   Auckland   Sydney
Mexico City   New Delhi   Hong Kong   Buenos Aires

Dolphins whistle and squeak.
They chirp and pop.

They make noises that sound
like clicks or claps.
Why do dolphins
make all these sounds?

Dolphins use sounds
to signal to other dolphins.
Each dolphin whistles in its own way.

No two dolphins sound the same.
A dolphin whistles over and over,
as if it is saying, "Here I am!"

7

Dolphins also show their feelings
with sounds.
An angry dolphin may squeak
or snap its jaw shut with a clap.
It may slap the surface of the water
with its fins or its tail.

Dolphins live underwater,

but they are not fish.

They are small whales.

Whales are mammals.

People are mammals too.

All mammals need to breathe air.

You use your mouth to breathe,
to eat, and to make sounds.
A dolphin uses its mouth to eat.
It uses the blowhole
on top of its head
to breathe and to make sounds.

A dolphin opens its blowhole
to breathe
but must keep it closed underwater.
Inside the blowhole
there are pockets called air sacs.

The dolphin makes a sound
by moving air
from one air sac to another.
If you hold the neck of a balloon
and let the air out slowly,
you can make a sound the same way.

A dolphin makes a clicking sound.

Then it listens for an echo.

A dolphin can hear the difference

between an echo bouncing off a rock

and an echo bouncing off a fish

or a shark or another dolphin.

This is called echolocation.

(Say it: ECK-oh-lo-CAY-shun.)

A dolphin can use echolocation

to find fish to eat

or to tell if a shark is nearby.

There are about 37 different
kinds of dolphins.
Most live in the ocean.
But some live in rivers
in China and India
and South America.
Most dolphins are gray
or black and white.
But two kinds of dolphins are pink!

Most dolphins live in groups
called schools.
Some schools have a few dolphins.
Others have hundreds.
Dolphins in a school help each other.
If one is hurt and can't swim,
other dolphins may lift it
to the water's surface
so it can breathe.

Dolphins like to touch
and pat each other with their fins.
They rub against each other.
They may swim side by side
with their fins touching
as if they are holding hands.

Baby dolphins are called calves.
Calves sometimes play with seaweed.
Or they swim up under a seagull
and knock it into the air.
Grown-up dolphins like to play too.

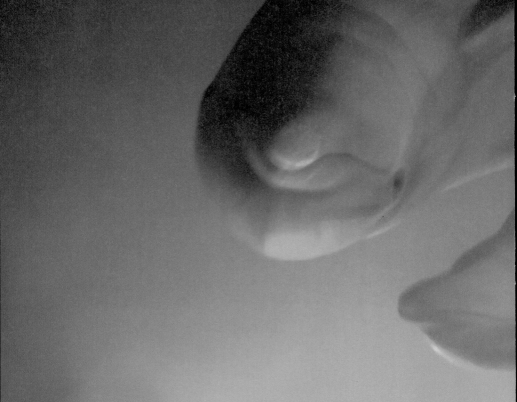

They ride the waves made by boats.
Calves stay with their mothers
for at least three years.
They drink their mother's milk.
Older calves can catch small fish.

Dolphins hunt for fish and squid.
They are also hunted.
Sharks and killer whales and people
kill dolphins for food.
People also catch dolphins
in fishing nets by mistake.

Once, thousands of dolphins were killed in tuna nets each year. When people heard about this, they stopped buying tuna fish. They asked the government to keep dolphins safe.

In the United States today,

people who fish for tuna

are not allowed to catch dolphins.

But dolphins are still in danger.

Trash dumped into the water

can make dolphins sick

and kill the fish that they eat.

When people put dams in rivers,

dolphins can't live there anymore.

Scientists go out in boats
to study wild dolphins.
They can tell the dolphins apart
by the fins on their backs.
Scientists count the dolphins
and follow them.

They find out what they eat
and how far they swim.
They try to understand the meanings
of the sounds that dolphins make.

Scientists learn
how we can help dolphins survive.
People helped to save dolphins
from tuna nets.

Now we must protect dolphins
from people who hunt them.
We must keep oceans
and rivers clean.

Then there will always be dolphins,
squeaking and whistling,
swimming and playing,
living in our world.

We can teach other people

why we need

to have sharks

in our world.